I0606212

DISCOVER ANCIENT CIVILIZATIONS

Ancient Egypt

by M.J. York

CAPSTONE VALUE LIBRARY
a capstone imprint

Published by Capstone® Value Library, an imprint of Capstone
1710 Roe Crest Drive, North Mankato, Minnesota 56003
capstonepub.com

Library of Congress Cataloging-in-Publication Data is available on the Library of Congress website
ISBN: 9798875306747 (hardcover)
ISBN: 9798875306778 (ebook PDF)

Summary: An exploration of the history and legacy of ancient Egypt.

Editorial Credits
Editor: Kellie M. Hultgren; Designer: Jennifer Walker; Production Specialist: Tori Abraham

Image Credits
Dreamstime: David Pillow, 13, Javarman, cover, Odyssei, 17, Takepicsforfun, 23, Vladimir Melnik, 21, Witold Ryka, 5; Shutterstock: ErenMotion, 9, muratart, 7

Printed and bound in the USA. 006585

Table of Contents

CHAPTER 1

Ancient Egypt

A great civilization arose on the banks of the Nile River in ancient times. The culture began taking shape about 5,000 years ago. Godlike kings called pharaohs commanded the farmers, builders, and soldiers. They built their most lasting **monuments**, the Great Pyramids, around 2,500 BCE.

Ancient Egypt lasted for thousands of years. The last independent ruler, Queen Cleopatra, died in 30 BCE. She lived closer to our time than to the building of the Great Pyramids. Today, the art and tombs of ancient Egypt still fascinate us.

Building of the Temple of Amun at Karnak began during the 1900s BCE.

CHAPTER 2

The River and the Desert

Egypt is shaped by desert and the Nile River. The Nile begins in the south and flows north. It runs into the Mediterranean Sea. The south is called Upper Egypt. It is dry, with mountains. The north is called Lower Egypt. There lies the Nile's **delta**. It is a large wedge of marsh and river draining into the sea. The Sahara desert lies to the west.

Ancient Egyptians lived in a narrow strip of fertile land next to the Nile. They relied on yearly floods for water and good soil for their farms.

Water from the Nile River made human life possible in ancient Egypt.

CHAPTER 3

The Pharaohs

In early times, the north and south had different cultures and rulers. Around 3100 BCE, one king united north and south. This began the time of the pharaohs with the first **dynasty**, or ruling family.

The pharaoh ruled Egypt. He was like a god on Earth. He made sure that temples were built. He made offerings and kept the gods happy. Then the crops would grow and the soldiers would win battles. The pharaohs' biggest building projects often were their tombs. The grandest were pyramids. There were many other styles too.

The Great Sphinx and pyramids at Giza are the most famous of the pharaohs' projects.

Running the Kingdom

Advisers helped the pharaohs rule. Ministers, **scribes**, architects, doctors, and others served the royal court. The kingdom was divided into **provinces**. Officials ran the provinces and collected taxes.

Most Egyptians were farmers. They gave most of their harvest to the local wealthy landowner. The landowner paid taxes with the grain. The government then used grain for trade or to pay workers in workshops. Extra grain was stored in **granaries** for years when the harvest was bad.

When the Nile flooded each year, the farmers could not work in the fields. Many then worked on royal tombs or projects.

CHAPTER 4

Daily Life

Most buildings were made of mud bricks. Farmers lived in simple homes. Palaces were built of mud bricks too. But they had tall columns and many decorations.

Average Egyptians lived mostly on barley bread and beer. Farmers raised cattle for the wealthy to eat. The richest people ate feasts of cheese, figs, cakes, pigeon, fish, and many other fine foods.

Most clothing was made of linen. Linen thread was made from flax, a widely grown crop. Both men and women wore knee-length skirts called kilts. Women also wore dresses. Wealthy men and women wore jewelry, wigs, and makeup.

Work and Women's Roles

Children usually learned the jobs of their parents. Future craftspeople and artists trained on the job. Children planning to be scribes or priests went to school. They studied from age 5 to age 16 or 17.

In many ways, women and men were treated equally. Unlike in many other ancient civilizations, women owned property. They could sign legal papers. They could hold most jobs. They worked as priestesses and scribes. They were artists and doctors. They ran businesses and farms.

A tomb painting shows scribe and astronomer Nakht (right) seated with his wife, Tawy, in front of a table of offerings.

Several queens held lots of power. Hatshepsut ruled for her stepson. Later she crowned herself pharaoh. She increased trade and built monuments. Egypt **prospered** under her. The most famous ruling queen was Cleopatra. She was a skilled and powerful ruler. After her death, Egypt was conquered by the Roman empire.

CHAPTER 5

Writing and Art

Egyptian writing is among the oldest in the world. The writing is called hieroglyphs. These symbols look like objects, animals, or shapes. They can stand for words or sounds. Egyptians wrote on papyrus. This paperlike material was made from papyrus reeds. Writing was carved in stone and painted on tomb walls too.

Egyptian painting also appears on tomb walls. It is known for its flat style. Faces are always drawn from the side. More important people were made larger than others. Paintings showed how ideas and people should relate to each other. They showed balance in the universe.

Boats, Building, and Other Advances

Boats were essential for trade and travel. The Nile River linked the north and south of the large kingdom. People had used boats on it since 6000 BCE or earlier. At first they were made from papyrus reeds. Later wooden boats had sails.

Egyptian architects and engineers were skilled builders. They used complicated math. Many of their temples and monuments are still standing today. The most famous are the Great Pyramids. They are made of giant stone blocks. Workers used ropes, rollers, and levers to raise the blocks up ramps.

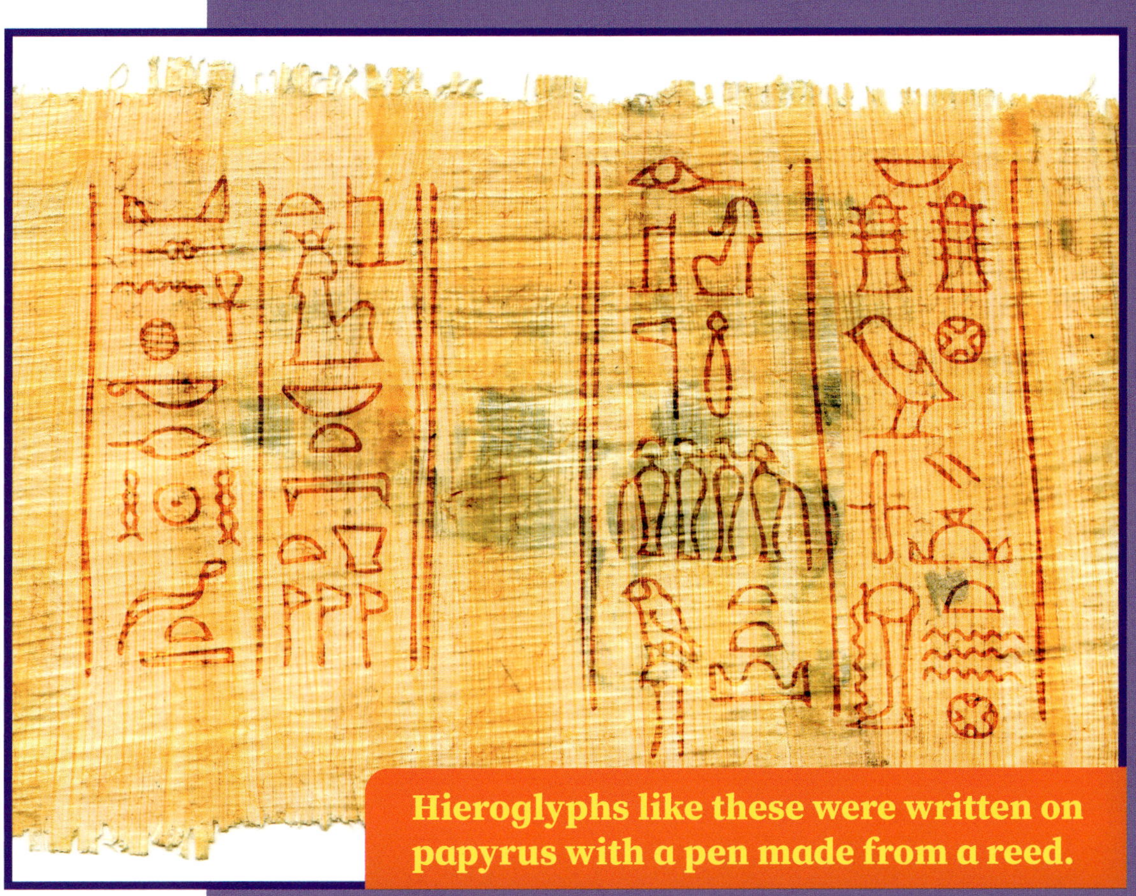

Hieroglyphs like these were written on papyrus with a pen made from a reed.

The Egyptians studied many sciences. They made advanced **irrigation** systems. They were among the first to use oxen to pull a plow. They watched the stars and made an accurate calendar. They practiced medicine and invented the first toothpaste!

CHAPTER 6

Gods and Goddesses and the Afterlife

Egyptians worshipped many gods and goddesses. The gods kept balance in the universe. Each was linked to different roles or ideas, such as good harvests, wisdom, or the sun. Many gods had a human form, an animal form, and a form with a human body and animal head.

The god Anubis helped the dead reach the afterlife. He was a jackal or had a jackal head. Osiris was god of the afterlife and the dead. Isis, his wife, was a mother goddess. She was also mother of Horus, the god of the pharaoh. Horus had a falcon head.

Temples had a statue of their god or goddess. Priests took care of the statue, washing it and making offerings of food. Festivals and feasts honored the god.

Reaching the afterlife was important to ancient Egyptians. Bodies were **mummified** and wrapped in cloth to be preserved. The wealthy were buried with treasure and everything they needed in life. This way they could be reborn in the afterlife.

A burial painting shows the god Anubis with the mummy of a tomb builder from Deir el-Medina.

CHAPTER 7

The Legacy of Egypt

The Egyptians wanted to live on after death. They built tombs and monuments to last. Many are still standing today. Near the pyramids at Giza, the Great Sphinx looks out over the desert. It has a lion body and a human head. Many pharaohs hid their tombs in the Valley of the Kings. There, archaeologists found the tomb of King Tutankhamun, or King Tut. Most tombs were looted in ancient times, but this tomb was still filled with gold and treasure.

Ancient Egypt flourished for thousands of years. Today we can still read the ancient Egyptians' names and stories. Their math, engineering, medicine, and farming became a foundation for later civilizations to build on.

Many historic discoveries remain to be made in the Valley of the Kings.

Glossary

delta (DEL-tuh)—sandy or muddy region where a river empties into a large body of water

dynasty (DYE-nuh-stee)—ruling family with several rulers holding power one after the other

granaries (GRAY-nuh-reez)—buildings where grain is stored

irrigation (ihr-uh-GAY-shuhn)—watering of farm and other land

monuments (MON-yuh-muhntz)—structures built to honor or remember someone

mummified (MUH-mih-fyde)—dried and preserved to not decay

prospered (PROSS-prd)—to be strong and flourishing

provinces (PROV-uhn-suhz)—regions into which a larger country or kingdom is divided

scribes (SKRYBZ)—people employed in reading and writing

Index